WALKING

Other Poetry Books By Nelson Ball

Certain Details: The Poetry Of Nelson Ball (WLU Press, 2017)
Walking With Catherine At Lake Erie (Shapes & Sounds Press, 2017)
You Can't Make The Sky A Different Blue (Big Pond Rumours, 2017)
Vole On A Roll (Shapes & Sounds Press, 2017)
Chewing Water (Mansfield Press, 2016)
Two Poems (press-press-pull/alabastine press, 2015)
This Close To Being A Tree (Monk Press, 2015)
Thirty Poems (Rubblestone Press, 2015)
Small Waterways (Apt. 9 Press, 2015)
Farmer's Dell Plaza (press-press-pull/alabastine press, 2015)
All And Everything (Laurel Reed Books, 2015)
Some Mornings (Mansfield Press, 2014)
You Must Look Hard To See What's There (press-press-pull, 2014)
Three-Letter Words (2nd edition, press-press-pull, 2014)
A Rattle Of Spring Frogs (Hamilton Arts & Letters, 2014, online)
Minutiae (Apt. 9 Press, 2014)
A Gathering (new edition, BookThug, 2014)
Orphans (Rubblestone Press, 2012)
The Continuous Present (Proper Tales Press, 2012)
In This Thin Rain (Mansfield Press, 2012)
Nine Poems (Rubblestone Press, 2011)
Three-Letter Words (Laurel Reed Books, 2006)
At The Edge Of The Frog Pond (The Mercury Press, 2004)
With Held (Laurel Reed Books, 2004)
Scrub Cedar (above/ground press, 2003)
A Gathering (Rubblestone Press, 2003)
Almost Spring (The Mercury Press, 1999)
Visitation (Rubblestone Press, 1998)
To Share That Yellow (fingerprinting inkoperated, 1998)
The Concrete Air (The Mercury Press, 1996)
Round Table (Letters, 1996)
Small Gardens (fingerprinting inkoperated, 1996)
Bird Tracks On Hard Snow (ECW Press, 1994)
Fifteen Poems (MindWare, 1994)
Sightings (Curvd H&z, 1992)
With Issa: Poems 1964-1971 (ECW Press, 1991)
Force Movements (2nd edition, Curvd H&z, 1990)
Round Stone (Weed/Flower Press, 1971)
Points Of Attention (Weed/Flower Press, 1971)
The Pre-Linguistic Heights (Coach House Press, 1970)
Water-Pipes And Moonlight (Weed/Flower Press, 1969)
Force Movements (Ganglia Press, 1969)
Sparrows (Weed/Flower Press, 1968)
Beaufort's Scale (Weed/Flower Press, 1967)
Room Of Clocks (Weed/Flower Press, 1965)

Books Edited

Konfessions Of An Elizabethan Fan Dancer by bpNichol (Coach House Books, 2004)
Frank Harrington's Kristmiss Book (The Mercury Press, 1993)

WALKING

Nelson Ball

Mansfield Press

a st^uart ross book

Library and Archives Canada Cataloguing in Publication

Ball, Nelson, 1942-, author
    Walking / Nelson Ball.

Poems.
ISBN 978-1-77126-164-7 (softcover)

    I. Title.

PS8503.A59W35 2017   C811'.6   C2017-905894-0

Editor for the press: Stuart Ross
Typesetting & cover design: Stuart Ross
Cover photo: Catherine Stevenson
Author photo: Laurie Siblock

The publication of *Walking* has been generously supported by
the Canada Council for the Arts and the Ontario Arts Council.

 Canada Council   Conseil des Arts
for the Arts   du Canada

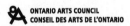 ONTARIO ARTS COUNCIL
CONSEIL DES ARTS DE L'ONTARIO

Mansfield Press Inc.
25 Mansfield Avenue, Toronto, Ontario, Canada M6J 2A9
Publisher: Denis De Klerck
www.mansfieldpress.net

Walking is not a sport.
　　　　—Frédéric Gros

Walking, you escape from the very idea of identity,
the temptation to be someone, to have a name and
a history.
　　　　— Frédéric Gros

The eternal child is one who has never seen anything
so beautiful, because he [or she] doesn't compare.
　　　　— Frédéric Gros

The setting sun goes down beside a bird.
　　　　—Wang Wei

Walking is to experience these quietly and humbly
insistent realities—the tree growing between rocks,
the watchful bird, the streamlet finding its course—
without expecting anything.
　　　　— Frédéric Gros

Sunlight cast back comes deep in the woods
and shines once again upon the green moss.
　　　　—Wang Wei

The reason elephants live so long is that they breathe slowly, and explore each breath completely.... Their basic theory is that all living creatures have an allotted number of breaths to live on.... Elephants have no respect for athletes. Way too much breathing! ... The mating season always demands enormous amounts of breathing: all that fighting and trumpeting. So the elephants take long walks and try to come up with more rational breathing techniques during mating, but this only makes them more excited, and they are breathing faster than ever. It's a terrible dilemma and they're not even close to solving it. They sigh heavily, and walk on, further and further into the dry savannah, lost in thought.

—Dag T. Straumsvåg

For Catherine Stevenson

Contents

I Employ "Whatever" In A Poem

Could my non-belief
in a higher power

account for my
sailing at speed

toward the end—
that wall of white light—

happy as a lark
writing poems about whatever?

Context Is Everything

Now that my emphysema
is problematic, I'm reluctant

to tell my friend
the sight of her

takes
my breath away

August 4, 2016

Catherine found a dead grackle
on my doorstep, below

the steel and plate glass front door.
On the glass I found two

tiny white translucent feathers
adhered by the root tips of their quills

wavering in place,
appearing enabled

for flight, with
or without their bird.

Next day we had
high winds driving heavy rain.

On the glass remains
a smudge

barely
perceptible.

December 24, 2016

Is it growing darker this early afternoon?
Am I losing my eyesight?

Are my eyeglasses dirty?

The sky is a bit darker.

World news is depressing.
My glasses are dirty.

Overheard

A
breeze

works

trees'
leaves

sounding

a river's
rapids

Fog

air
occupying

its
shadow

Excuse For Writing Short Poems

My jottings
that develop into poems

are written
in a small notebook

I carry
in my pocket

In My Time

short
trees

grew

very
tall

Perplexed

Last week I was writing a poem about my friend Catherine.
Soon after we met three years ago, I developed

a crush on her. Which is odd, given my age,
her youth, my poor health, her little kids,

and her partner Clayton. Perhaps
I wanted to be young again. How young?

The age of Clayton? Or her kids?
To be honest, I don't know. She visited

last week while I was in hospital
receiving restorative lung therapy. She brought tea,

a Laughing Buddha, and lavender.
I told her about the poem.

She gave me a hug.
I came home rejuvenated.

Your Hands Are Too Cold!

Tall, thin people have cold hands and feet—
that's my theory. I'm tall and thin

and I had to warm my hands
before canoodling with Barbara

and further, keep my feet
away from her while we slept.

Barbara was little, short—
warm all over.

Walking On Air

I have a stationary Home Oxygen Concentrator, a cannula,
and a fifty-foot hose

that follows me like a snail's trail
along the hallway, in and out of rooms

and gets underfoot. I'm thrilled
by my extra energy,

tell myself a joke
while stepping on the hose.

Showboat

A small bird
struts

across
the parking lot

head
high

tail
down

Signs: Late Fall

Fallen
leaves

wind
driven

flatten
against

the wire
fence

Signs: Early Spring

Flattened
leaves

still
hug

the wire
fence

Across Fields

Distant
indistinct

woodlots
drift

dark
islands

in a lake
of snow

Gifts From Catherine

for Catherine Stevenson

It is difficult finding appropriate gifts for some people.
I'm one of those, having a house already filled with books.

Catherine, defying the odds, has given me two memorable volumes:
Patience & Fortitude: Wherein A Colorful Cast

Of Determined Book Collectors, Dealers, And Librarians
Go About The Quixotic Task Of Preserving A Legacy

by Nicholas A. Basbanes (Perennial, 2003). It includes
a lengthy and accurate description of Peter B. Howard

my late colleague and friend, of Serendipity Books
in Berkeley, California. One of Peter's stories involves

handling, on consignment, the paper archive 1910-1940
of the California chapter of the NAACP. It was found

awaiting disposal at a local landfill in 1991 and placed with Peter
who sold it to the Bancroft Library, University of California.

The archive records the growing self-awareness
of a long-suppressed group of people.

The other book from Catherine is *Quiet: The Power*
Of Introverts In A World That Can't Stop Talking

by Susan Cain (Broadway, 2013). The description on page 103,
of "high-reactive" children who pay "alert attention

to people and things," accounts for how and why
I perceive and write the way I do. These two books

have been perfect gifts. Now, joining the books as a perfect gift
is a load of 100 rolls of toilet paper.

I asked Catherine to pick them up for me. She did, then
refused to accept payment, saying "It's your Christmas present—

it's something I know you want." I thanked her.
They were "on sale," but not cheap—

Royale™ Original, "double-rolls," 2-ply, 253 sheets per roll.
I wanted this many rolls because I'm shut in until spring

and my desire to survive to use them all
may subdue, through a difficult winter, my advancing COPD.

Catherine encourages my effort to live longer. She is frugal
with her money so I am touched by this gift. I am frugal

with things, not wanting to waste anything. When I buy
a loaf of fresh bread, I give her the remaining loaf.

She feeds it to her growing sons
who, although trim, eat largely.

Suzan's Boot Laces

to Suzan Yates, who otherwise
manifests a brilliant mind

Suzan's
a thrift store fashion statement

of more savvy
than women shopping on New York's Fifth Avenue

but, unnoticed, the laces
of her knee-high, black leather boots are untied.

Tie the laces,
Suzan!

Your brain
is too precious

to thud
against the sidewalk.

The Pen

for Kate Belair

Kate gave me a small wrapped box for Christmas.
I assumed chocolates. It was a luxury pen!

Cross brand, Edge model,
"Octane Green Rollerball"

I couldn't get the point to protrude,
found instructions on the Internet.

Tiny letters on the barrel read:
MANULIFE / PRIVATE / INVESTMENT / POOL.

Aha—
from her husband Jon's stock of gifts for clients.

It's a treasure.
How else can a minor poet

receive a luxury pen
from a major financial institution?

I revised poems on Christmas night.
Wrote new ones next day.

Catherine

It is sweet
saying your name

from a deep well
of wistfulness

a rhythmic
whisper

almost
a sweet sickness

I Propel Myself

I squatted low to fetch a book
from an awkward-to-reach shelf.

In attempting to rise, I propelled myself
backwards, rather than

upward, due to my weak leg muscles.
I grabbed a shelf, landed

safely on my bum, not
my head. Catherine took my hand,

helped me to stand, get
my breath, stop shaking.

Was this deliberate, in order
to hold hands with her?

Shallow Creek

Water
wiggles through

shallow
passages

miniature
rapids

minnows
tadpoles

Prelude

Clouds
like cotton batting stained

dark
grey

near
black

and
worried

Peculiar

Like a dust devil
in an otherwise still, cold day

snow, swirling
five feet wide

twice
my height

Birds

I don't
understand the birds

can't they
stay in one place

mid-distance
from where they summer

and where they winter,
some place

mild
every day?

Short Take: United States

Hand over heart
they pray and sing

renew the right
to shoot themselves

of course
in self-defence

Canada's Capital Opportunities

Pat Moore
says there is worldwide

a shortage of sand
for construction projects

in tourism-directed landscaping—
new beaches, new islands.

Ecosystems in some regions have collapsed
due to the theft of sand from riverbanks and beaches

taken by locals during the night—
sold to the multinationals.

Brings new meaning
to Alberta oil sands extraction—

take the sand
leave the oil

elsewhere giant grinders
could harvest

the rock
of the Laurentian Shield.

Four-Letter Words

for Suzan Yates

Suzan read "My Doctor"—my poem
that closes with "thud, thud, thud"—

said it reminded her
of when she was twelve—her mother

gave her four books to enlighten her
about dating, the birds and the bees.

Suzan, a sophisticate, nose in the air,
trotted off

books in hand,
muttering "buzz, buzz, buzz."

My Doctor

to Dr. John W. McDonald, with gratitude

Today's visit with my doctor was businesslike, perhaps
something on his mind that didn't involve me.

He keeps me on a short leash, a visit every four to six weeks.
We have a deal, he keeps me alive, I continue

to write poems and give him my books. I like this.
He likes my poems. They are "in the moment" he says.

That's a wonderful response. I'm pleased.
Today he's brisk, asking only the essential questions,

then moving to listen with his stethoscope to my heart and lungs.
I've been concerned, although he doesn't seem to be,

by my enlarged heart, working hard to overcome
the shortage in my respiratory system of oxygen.

I asked "How does my heart sound?" He replied
"thud-thud-thud." That's all he said.

Listening To Michael And Allison Silently Read

I focus
on breathing, the cool

sensuality of air
moving in to the lungs

listening
while Michael and Allison read typescripts

the periodic sound
when they fold over a sheet

accentuating
the silence

those slight sounds
that carefully turned paper makes

Signs: Early May

Rain
persists

non-
stop

gathering
in ditches

road-
side

puddles
deepen

acquire
geese

Retail Wording

Retail clerks in this town
add "at all" or "today" or both

to the end of an interrogatory sentence
spoken to a customer.

It results in questions such as
"Are you a senior at all today?"

My Memorial Stone

I don't want one.
I don't want to die.

Not yet, anyway.
If I die in the following manner

then I'll have a stone
with this inscription:

"He died on the toilet"
memorializing the indignity.

Lines In Spring

The space outside my kitchen window
occupied by the blue spruce

fills now
with multiple flight paths

of tension-filled birds
driven by lust and maternal instinct

Early Morning

My neighbour
with his old car avoids

a needed tune-up, rather
sits in his car

revving the engine for ten minutes,
more or less, until it runs smoothly,

more or less, seems
like hours.

Update On Noah's Yacht

Noah's
yacht

in the field
replaced by

a pick-up
truck

Unfettered Capitalism

would shut down
our imaginations

that we might
spend our lives

watching TV
buying things

cleaning
things

Catherine Visits

for Catherine Stevenson

III

Catherine asked if I'd had a good week.
"I had a lot of fun" I replied

"I played with words,
I don't like people."

She said
"That sounds like a poem."

IV

My friend Catherine
visits often, we talk

drink tea, she
says things I steal—

shape
into poems

V

Catherine spent the afternoon here
to avoid being in another place.

We talked and read, a quiet visit, and
exhausted from the sleeplessness of her children,

she curled into the wing chair
and slept for most of an hour.

I watched her face. She
snored quietly. I was tired from hours of talk

with Suzan the day before, some of it
complex and intense. I lay back

in the other chair
and slept.

VI

Your presence in my present
is a birthday gift to me

your
spirit

our
talk

your
hugs—

your
aliveness

infuses
mine.

VII

You gave me
the prototype of your feltie bird.

I named it
The Bird.

Poetry critic
James McDonald

commented
"It looks like a bird:

the wings
are great" he said

"the feet
are perfect."

VIII

I found on the floor
an elastic band

with a single hair
wound around it

it fell out
on your previous visit

I'm keeping it

Signage

"God
has thought

about you
today."

Names

Petermann Island, named
for German cartographer August Heinrich Petermann

has a cove discovered January first nineteen oh nine
by the Fourth French Antarctic Expedition

and named Port-Circoncision, or
in English, Port Circumcision

honouring the Feast of the Circumcision
celebrated on January first.

Perhaps in French Petermann
is less suggestive than in English

or they might have named it
Port Glory or Glory Bay

Should I
an English Canadian named Ball

make an issue
of this?

My *Suzuki Beane*

The problem in thinking you are finished with a book
is that years later you may fervently wish you had kept it.

Marty Ahvenus and I were in love with Suzuki Beane in the sixties.
I was reminded of the little beatnik three times this year:

a drawing by Barbara Klunder; the explorer in *Sidewalk Flowers*;
and my expanding awareness of a child's perceptions.

I purchased a replacement of my long-lost book.
The cheapest decent copy

of the paperback edition
cost more than 150 dollars!

I paid for it!

Allen Ginsberg Flirted With My Little Brother

My brother was staying with me at Bathurst Street
on a short break from his first-year university studies—

aimed toward chemical engineering. Victor
brought Allen Ginsberg who was visiting

Coach House Press, a ten-minute walk from my place.
I expected talk about small presses, the poetry scene,

but Ginsberg focused on my brother, asking him
about school, his goals, employment,

etc., etc., etc., etc. ... This was when in a NYC automat
Ginsberg bought a 55¢ sandwich for Patti Smith,

chatted with her, asked if she were a boy or a girl.
That's how they met. They became lifelong friends.

Recently my brother said he was naive at that age,
didn't know who Allen Ginsberg was, nor

even now know that he had met him,
was unaware a man had flirted with him.

I began reading Ginsberg's poems while a student
in secondary school. They were among my favourites.

Brantford

He dove off the sidewalk
onto West Street, in front

of a police car, then dry-swam
failing to escape the officers

released next day, sobered
to restart the new year

Cannula

is not a contemporary word
like thingie or thingamajig

it's from seventeenth-century Latin
rooted in Greek

means
"small reed"—

a friendly word, soft
like canoodle

delivers oxygen
to my nose

March

A day
overcast and cold

the dark woodlot
seems distant

Lightning: August 2, 2015

Light
enough to illuminate
a city—

the bang
splits
air

Noah's Yacht

Next to the property
of the Brethren of Early Christianity

(located between the villages
of Washington and Drumbo)

is a small farm
with a brick farmhouse

and sitting alone
in a nearby field

a small
yacht

Lawns In Seaforth

The nicest grounds
win horticultural society prizes

lawns with kids' toys spread about—
that's okay

but an old car rusting
on the front lawn

no licence plate
tires flat—

that's
an

other
story

Mary And The Alligators

for Mary Neff

I don't understand why
my sister travels to South Carolina

to ride a bike and golf
among the alligators.

Patrick says alligators are lazy—
one simply walks around them.

Then I see a photograph of Mary
holding a small one like a puppy.

Birds

for Lucas

Birds
in spring

pick
up

sticks
and string

leave me
wondering

do they
freak out

at Lucas's yarn bombings
saying

"Wow!
enough for two nests

and
a sweater!"

Isaiah And I

for Heather Smith

My friend Heather
told me Isaiah, age two

waves to my building
when they drive past.

She said he prefers
girls as playmates.

So did I
when I was little.

Still
do.

I Don't Know The Rules

for Calantha Babineau

Kemeny and Laurie took me to a rugby game this afternoon—
High School Senior Girls—

Calantha on the Brantford team.
They played Paris in Paris.

Kemeny says they tackle roughly
I think he used the word "savage."

But mostly they run, zigzag, at lightning speed
passing the ball, back and forth, fast actions

of perfectly coordinated play
that I watched in awe.

One team won. I don't know which.
That doesn't matter.

My Career In Education

Two years in kindergarten. I remember
folding sheets of paper into airplanes

that landed on a pipe
emerging from the furnace.

This church basement was our classroom
until a new school was built.

I don't remember classmates. My mother said
a neighbour girl walked me to school.

Her last name was Winter.
I remember the name, not the girl.

I became a mediocre student
except in physics and social psychology.

Global Warming: Northward Travelling Asian Carp

I was seventeen years old in 1959
at a Junior Forest Ranger camp near Thessalon.

Our leader, Jamie, was probably twenty-one
but he seemed like an adult.

The work was horrible—
planting trees under the hot sun

sucking on salt tablets
then going for a swim in the nearby lake.

Herbie was the sophisticate—
from London, Ontario, while

the rest of us were from small towns
and villages. Herbie was a clown

but perhaps prescient. He would struggle to stand
in the shallow water, dragging his leg

shouting, Jamie, Jamie, help—
an alligator caught my leg.

Industrial Farming

Industrial
farming

produces

vacant
farmhouses

Selling Rock In Canada

When I was young, stones were everywhere—

on farmers' fields they would break ploughs and shoulders
on roads they would break your car.

A friend's father lent us his 1932 Chevrolet
to fetch stones from the lakeshore

and fill holes in the long muddy road
leading to our families' cottages.

We were too young to be licensed—
this was exciting, driving on our own.

My uncle Harold had a stone boat on his farm—
two logs parallel, a metre or more apart,

topped by rough boards on which to pile stones.
This was dragged by horses or a tractor

carrying the stones to the edges of a field.
It took several men to move large boulders

less common in this region of southwestern Ontario.
The piles at the edges of fields were snake habitat.

Anyone needing stones could take what they wanted.
At the cottage we gathered rocks as anchors for docks

smaller, flat ones for pathways. Fifty years ago
when I first became aware that people

bought rocks for their lawns I was flummoxed.
Why not go out and pick them up yourself?

Our country is half rock.
Preposterous. I still think that.

Thin Girls

This summer some girls wear
ankle-length dresses, at least

the skinny ones with long legs do
who when seen from the side

disappear

Futility

Washing
the
infant's
face

or
the
truck's
tires

Hatching

p   e

      e   k

      p

A Happy Life

Coffee
each
morning

until

the
day
after

Spring

Birds
and people

scavenge
sticks

for
nests

tidy
lawns

Novelette: The Kettle

Patrick and Anita say their gas range
heats the kitchen
before it boils water

Waiting ...

...

waiting ... for ...

...

waiting ... for ... water ...

...

waiting ...

...

waiting ...

Anomaly: The Pasture

short
grasses

tall
thistles

Someone

The Mossop house
where Mother was born

a farmhouse on the Bronson Line
south of Bayfield

has been vacant
for thirty years

but someone
mows the lawn

An Analogy To American Foreign Policy

as found on Wikipedia, August 24, 2015

Tommie Woodward, 28, male, July 3, 2015, was killed
in the early morning at a Southeast Texas marina.

Woodward ignored warnings not to swim in the water
because of the danger of alligators;

his last known words were
"Fuck the alligators."

As Time Goes By

Vacant
barns

weaken
collapse

rolled
wire fencing rusts

cows
gone

now
corn

the bigger
industry

Pursuit

Birds do odd things
in love and lust

whomp
against kitchen windows:

as we say
"Knock yourself out!"

Poop Flingers

Farmers
fling poop with machines

it's mechanical
not emotional

Chimpanzees
on the other hand

throw poop
at people

and
laugh

Question On A Dark Night

Where
does
the
light
go
after
the
car
is
gone
?

Sidetracked

I march into a room, pause
look around, ask myself

"What was I looking for?
Why am I here?"

Today, I add
"Why are any of us here?"

Finally:
"Where are we?"

Dear Catherine

I met you on a mild day in October
at the Adelaide Hunter Hoodless Homestead

while I walked the grounds, and you
seated at a picnic table

were writing an essay
on the conservation and restoration of materials.

We spoke, you were gracious,
suggesting I return for a tour.

You, young and beautiful, I
was shy about returning, then

after visits and conversation
my adolescent self was smitten.

I told you this and was surprised
you were not alarmed

but gently informed me
of your relationship with Clayton.

I had a goal for this poem.
What was it?

Perhaps to thank you for your friendship,
for my restoration.

I Have A Young Friend

for Catherine; remembering Barbara

I like to look
in her face

when we talk
I watch her think

I listen while
she circles a topic

describing
coaxing forth

meaning
ideas

Barbara
spoke this way

circling
coaxing

finding
meaning

I have been
so fortunate

in love
and in friendship

Signs: February 28

A beach ball
rolls

across
the yard

Poop Factor

A 4,000 year old plant virus
no longer active anywhere in the world

discovered thawed in the arctic
in 700 year old caribou poop

On The Shiny Surface Of The "Battleship Linoleum" Floor

A
fly

long-
legged

walks
atop

its
shadow

Leaves Leave

Colour
leaves the tree

in spring
through summer

spectacular
in fall

until
they fall

leaving
branches bare

On The Front Steps

I see
an ant—

a black spot
in motion—

then several,
ones—

then,
many

Warblers

Roadside
they fly, steep

dippers
and

rapid
risers

all
at

top
speed

For Catherine Stevenson

with thanks for this story

After peeing all over
near the toilet

the seven year old
seriously advised his mother

"You know, penises for boys
are very hard to control."

Bugs In The Bathroom

Catherine rescues small animals
removes them from danger—

turtles from the road
bugs from the bathroom.

She carried a large hairy black spider
by one leg to the backyard.

Her children freaked out—
the youngest, terrified,

wanted to know exactly
where she had placed it—

how far from the house,
the precise location.

This boy is not afraid
of snakes, when younger

he called them "nakes."
Spiders are his monster.

Lunch Today

thanks, Suzan Yates

To my bowl of Bran Buds, I add from Suzan
a peach muffin, more like a cupcake

she calls it
an "imposter"

a bit of table cream
ice cream

K

for Catherine Stevenson

K may be spoken as a gentle question.
Or assertively, as a command.

It's often spoken by young mothers
to children and old people.

K may be seen as an abbreviation of ok and okay
but ok doesn't need an abbreviation. So, k is a new word.

Ok is a long-standing word. Years ago
it was an acronym, written O.K.

It stood for orl korrect, a jocular alternative to all correct,
used by nineteenth-century journalists and humourists.

It was popularized as a slogan
in the U.S. election campaign of 1840

reproducing the initials of Old Kinderhook,
the birthplace and nickname

of President Martin Van Buren,
who was seeking re-election.

I learned the complexity of spoken k
listening to Catherine speak to her child

and to me, one of her old people.
Van Buren lost the 1840 presidential election.

Walking With Catherine At Lake Erie

to Catherine Stevenson

I

At Port Ryerse
Catherine took photos of me

liberated by my "wings"—
the portable oxygen concentrator.

We took a short walk. I was slow
but did not gasp—

the first time
in months.

II

While Catherine and I road-tested
my ability to walk, she told me

about the probability of dying
on the toilet.

I walked slowly, but
didn't gasp—

couldn't
stop laughing.

III

I watched Catherine compose a photograph
of a beached blue and red rowboat

backed by a floating rowboat
with a pale yellow-green interior

in a cove, edged by a stand
of brown and green rushes.

She moved in closer, then out
to each side, finally sitting

on the trunk
of a fallen tree.

Her exploration in looking and seeing
is analogous

to catching words
to make a poem.

IV

I discovered that, despite my difficulty breathing,
I'm still able to walk on sand.

From this Normandale lakeshore wilderness
I could see the industrial complex of the Nanticoke-

coal-fired-electrical-generating-station. Then
I watched Catherine examine and select

small pieces of driftwood that she
will arrange in the nest-like clusters

that lurk within her Waterford home
to surprise the curious explorer.

V

Catherine sat on the ground
taking photos of a little blue flying stick

hovering, touching
the green stalk of a tall grass

holding its place
by the blur of its colourless wings

beautiful
primary and secondary colours

but the blur—
no words for that.

VI

I was talking about how my body measures,
by shortness of breath, energy expended

for activities, such as eating,
which until recently had me gasping.

My greatest surprise has been using the toilet
where simply peeing without extra oxygen

required rest on a chair
on exiting the bathroom.

Catherine was not surprised. Her mother
tells the story of a relative who declared

his intent to die with his boots on—
he died on the toilet.

His nephew found him, put on his boots.
Catherine's mother says dying on the toilet

is more common than people realize.
She's a retired nurse.

VII

Catherine thinks she is more likely
to go this way. I think I am—

right-side heart enlargement. One of us
will find out about one of us.

Notes

This book is dedicated also to the memory of Barbara Caruso (1937–2009), my wife and soulmate. She was a visual artist and writer. We were a team, together for forty-four years. We had memorable walks on the Campbell Trail in Ayr.

I attempted to resume writing poetry in 1986, having ceased in 1972 so I could focus on my bookselling business. When we moved from Toronto to rural Paris, Ontario, in 1985, my pent-up desire to write about the rural landscape was overwhelming, yet I found it difficult to do.

I felt an invisible barrier denying me access. I wondered if I could become one with a landscape, as a means to understanding it. I considered lying in a field and writing about what I could examine closely, the patch of ground where I lay.

Could I become one with a field? This frightened me. I wondered if it was a death wish. I spent nearly two years in a state of anxiety, wondering how to write the landscape, how to convey an essence of fieldness. It was a powerful ache.

I came to realize that the wholeness of a landscape was more than I could encompass in a poem. I proceeded to examine and write about the smallest details. Would writing small details produce meaningful poems? Would they convey some significance of the whole? I would try.

It took time before I got beyond superficial description and began to feel I was producing depictions that revealed meaning. I view the latter as a spiritual experience. Something of this appears to occur in aboriginal cultures but not in Western religion. There seem to be parallels in Eastern religion and philosophy.

I was elated by what Norwegian poet Dag T. Straumsvåg recently wrote to Stuart Ross about my poems. He wrote:

Like Olav H. Hauge, [Ball] seems to be writing from inside the landscape, rather than like a tourist looking in from the outside. I love it. Tom Hennen does that, too. Ball seems to be more minimalistic than Tom and Hauge, but otherwise they seem to have a lot in common.

This characterization recognizes an occasionally noticed aspect of my poetry—the particular centre that coalesces from close observations.

My thinking and my observational and writing skills had been honed by numerous activities during my hiatus from poetry. Hence the experience of perceiving and writing was qualitatively different compared to the earlier years. I can't otherwise account for why my earlier poems didn't guide me back into writing poetry.

Walking has been integral to my writing. Most often I walk alone. I stop frequently to observe and make notes. When I walk alone, my identity falls away. The absence of identity allows an intense absorption of what I see. What I see becomes more real than I am. It is a transcendent-like experience.

Prior to Barbara's death, I walked in the Dickson Wilderness Area and the Cambridge To Paris Rail Trail. When Barbara died, friends showed me some of the numerous walking trails and paths in Brant, Oxford, and Norfolk Counties and in the Regions of Waterloo and Hamilton.

Mary Neff and Jackie Morris took me respectively to the Short Hills Trail near Welland and the Dundas Valley Conservation Area. I explored wilderness trails at Varna. Patrick Campbell and I climbed along the Niagara escarpment at Spencer Gorge and explored the shorelines of the Nith and Grand Rivers. We found lightning-struck trees in the dense and humid Chesney Wilderness Area near Drumbo. Kememy Babineau and I fought our way through the undergrowth along the Grand. Patricia Moore and I walked the Rail Trail almost daily for several months. I frequently walked the grounds of the Adelaide Hunter Hoodless Homestead near St. George.

My walks alone were long in time and short in distance. I experienced an extended period of grieving following Barbara's death, despite my frequent walks with and without companions. As the grief subsided, my loneliness intensified. I was certain I would never again be happy. Then came months of chemo and radiation treatment for throat cancer.

I met Catherine Stevenson at the end of this period, in October 2011. We began and continue wonderful conversations. Her presence in my life is magical, providing emotional and spiritual sustenance, and profound joy. We have taken memorable walks at Waterford and at Lake Erie.

I chose the epigraphs in the front of this book to link walking, breathing, observation, perception, and meditation.

The Epigraphs

Frédéric Gros: *A Philosophy of Walking* by Frédéric Gros. Translated by John Howe. London, Verso, 2015.

Wang Wei (699–761): in *An Anthology Of Chinese Literature: Beginnings to 1911*. Edited and translated by Stephen Owen. New York & London, W. W. Norton, 1997.

"The setting sun goes down beside a bird" from Wang Wei's poem "Written On Climbing The Small Terrace Of Pei Di." This is said to be the earliest occurrence in Chinese poetry that accepts this visual image without noting that the sun is a distant body. It presents the sun and bird on a flat plane. In my opinion this is an early occurrence of a modernist perception.

"Sunlight cast back..." is from Wang Wei's poem "Deer Fence."

Dag Straumsvåg: Excerpts from "Postcard With Elephants," translated by Louis Jenkins in Dag T. Straumsvåg's *The Lure-Maker From Posio*. Translated by Robert Hedin and Louis Jenkins. Minnesota, Red Dragonfly Press, 2011.

"Allen Ginsberg Flirted With My Little Brother"
The flirt occurred in 1970. My brother Joe, eight years my junior, is now a retired petroleum engineer who lives in rural Alberta with his wife, Pam, and enjoys time with their four grandchildren as often as possible.

Barbara and I lived in a third-floor flat on Bathurst near Bloor Street in Toronto from 1968 to 1973. The flat housed our living quarters, Barbara's painting studio, and my small press, Weed/Flower Press.

During that time Victor Coleman was the editor at Coach House Press. House of Anansi Press had published Ginsberg's book *Airplane Dreams* in 1968. Coach House published *Iron Horse* in 1972.

Patti Smith describes first meeting Ginsberg in the early 1970s in her wonderful autobiography *Just Kids*, HarperCollins, 2010.

Ginsberg's poems were not in my school texts; I found them in the Dell paperback anthology titled *The Beat Generation and the Angry Young Men* (1959).

"Catherine Visits VII"
A feltie is a three-dimensional construction made of felt. Catherine makes feltie animals including birds, bears, foxes, rabbits, cats, and a wolf. She designs her felt constructions.

"Hatching"
This poem is dedicated to Kemeny Babineau.

"Listening To Michael And Allison Silently Read"
Michael Casteels and Allison Chisholm visited by coincidence just at the time I had completed writing the autobiographical essay that serves as an afterword to my selected poems, *Certain Details*. I was seeking responses, and they read it during their visit. Their responses were positive. I was pleased, and I'm grateful to them.

"My *Suzuki Beane*"
Suzuki Beane is the main character who narrates an eponymously titled book written by Sandra Scoppettone and illustrated by Louise Fitzhugh. It was published by Doubleday in 1961 and issued as a mass-market paperback by MacFadden Books in 1962.

Marty Ahvenus operated the Village Book Store in Toronto on Gerrard Street West, a place I frequented and where I served my apprenticeship as an emerging bookseller. Marty was a friend to poets.

Barbara Klunder's cartoon character, Little Rude Riding Hood, comments astutely on the real nature of the Olympic Games: "Oh, let's face it. The Olympics are *always* a real estate project, disguised as a freak show. Yup."

Sidewalk Flowers is a Governor General's Award–winning wordless storybook by JonArno Lawson and Sydney Smith.

Catherine Stevenson's youngest son is the unidentified child.

"Names"
August Heinrich Petermann (1822–1878) was a leading cartographer. He was born in Germany and worked primarily there and in England, where he was a member of the Royal Geographical Society of London and was appointed by Queen Victoria her "physical geographer-royal."

Petermann is noted for technical innovations in mapmaking and for his teaching. He was masterful in working with information from multiple sources to produce a single map. He published many maps and articles. He was not a traveller.

Petermann Island in the Antarctic is one of numerous features named in his honour. It is a small, rocky, partly ice-covered island that is home to a breeding colony of gentoo penguins and is a tourist destination.

"Noah's Yacht"
The Brethren of Early Christianity was founded by Julius Kubassek (1893–1961), an emigrant from Hungary. He was an atheist as a youth. As a soldier in the Great War, he was horrified by its cruelty. He

deserted. While hiding on a farm in Czechoslovakia in 1919, he read the New Testament scripture and was smitten by the simple religion portrayed.

He gathered followers while visiting among Hutterites as he travelled across Canada before settling near Glen Morris, Ontario, in 1939. They moved to their current location in 1941.

They were in conflict with the local populations and government over, among other things, their lack of nationalism and the education of their children. They were accepted peacefully following the end of WWII.

Today they thrive as a commune producing many products: from bedding and textile products, to furniture, plastics, and metalworks including industrial and commercial machinery parts and tools.

Historical information in this note was derived from Peter G. Clark's *The Brethren of Early Christianity: A Study of a World Rejecting Sect*, Thesis (M.A.), McMaster University, Hamilton, Ontario, 1967.

"Perplexed"
I received restorative lung therapy in April 2014.

"Walking With Catherine At Lake Erie"
Written October 9–15, 2016, based on excursions in 2015 and 2016. A cluster poem celebrating our wonderful conversations. Further dedicated to two more Fox family storytellers: Catherine's mother, Susan Stevenson, and Susan's brother, actor David Fox.

Normandale is a quiet village on the shore of Lake Erie. In the early 1800s it was the location of a large foundry that produced farm implements, stoves, and smaller utensils including kettles, pots, and pans from local bog iron ore. It closed around 1850. Clayton Barker found an area with pieces of slag indicating the location of the foundry. In Europe, bog iron smelting predates the Roman era.

A Note From Catherine Stevenson

Nelson and I met at a time when we were both in the midst of very different, but profoundly difficult, transitions. He was mourning the loss of his beloved Barbara; I was wading through the end of my marriage.

The Adelaide Hunter Hoodless Homestead, where I was curator, was my sanctuary. It is located in the midst of the rolling hills near St. George, Ontario. Nelson was managing his grief through long walks. One day, he walked through the Homestead grounds where I sat working on an essay: our sanctuaries aligned.

Since then my life has settled, and I have been able to identify some of the elements that help me feel healthier and more contented. Things that narrow my focus and enable me to exist in the present.

The photo on the cover of this book was a result of this new mindfulness. While driving, I noted fleeting changes in light and colour as the setting sun warmed the autumn fields. I stopped, exited the car, strolled, and contemplated. In moments, the setting sun transformed the straw-covered folds of soil from gold to deep red to purple. Walking, I became part of a living, changing place that I would otherwise have only witnessed for a second through the windshield.

I have described my friendship with Nelson as an ongoing conversation. In "Catherine Visits I," he captures its essence: "here she will // speak words / onto the still air // where / they breathe // and we / look at them." And, as Stuart Ross has said, there is no separation between the world of Nelson Ball's poetry and the world of Nelson himself. Just as his poem is born of his willingness to observe without judgement, time with Nelson is filled with the same gentle focus.

With Nelson, I have learned to wait, to watch, to breathe, and to notice. He is a gift to me.

Catherine Stevenson
Waterford, August 15, 2017

A Note From Dag T. Straumsvåg

I first came across Nelson Ball's work two years ago, in a small Canadian magazine called *Hardscrabble*. Four short poems of stunning clarity and detail. Descriptive, simple poems, and yet mysterious. As I read more of his work, I became increasingly impressed. His detailed observations—from walks in the wild, from a car window, from small-town streets, from inside his house—are first-class.

The inherent mystery and complexity of all things is best presented in a clear and precise language. Nelson may be a relative of Askeladden in the Norwegian folk tale "The Princess No One Could Silence," who notices little things along the way that his travelling companions are too busy to notice or can't recognize the value of.

In many of Nelson's poems, something extraordinary is going on; he does not discriminate between the things he observes—a fly dying on its hind legs, an empty parking lot with the odour of skunk, the busy ant highways under the bark of a dead spruce, the darkening sky before rain. All are given the same careful attention. He is documenting what's happening around him, without passing judgment, without grading importance. Like the late, great Norwegian poet Olav H. Hauge, it is as if Nelson is writing from inside the landscape, rather than like a tourist looking in from the outside.

Although the majority of poems I have read by Nelson are nature poems, I don't think it is correct to label him a "nature poet." His body of work is too varied for such a label, and among his best work are beautiful love poems, moving poems of loss and grief, and funny poems, and he has written some of the finest friendship poems I have ever read.

As I kept reading his work, I started writing my own short poems, not consciously trying to write like him, but, inspired, trying to learn from him. A few of those poems eventually ended up in a chapbook called *Nelson*. His poems have reconnected me with silence, nature's silence, "the silence that lives in the grass/on the underside of each blade," to quote another Norwegian poet, Rolf Jacobsen.

Years ago, I was going for a walk in the woods, when all the birds and insects suddenly grew completely silent around me. Then, seconds later, they resumed their chirping and buzzing. It was stunning. That brief moment, when all my senses awakened as something remarkable was happening and not happening at the same time, will always stay with me: thousands of winged creatures simultaneously stopped making sounds and then simultaneously started again. Many of Nelson's poems are like that moment: quiet, unexpected, intensely alive, clear and inexplicable, precious.

Dag T. Straumsvåg
Trondheim, August 17, 2017

Acknowledgements

Most of these poems were written from 2015 to 2017. Drafts have had numerous readers offering suggestions and support. I'm grateful to all of you, including Cameron Anstee, Kemeny Babineau, Liz Ball, Clayton Barker, Kate Belair, Anita Campbell, Patrick Campbell, Larry Cowan, Brian David Johnston, Trisha Little, James McDonald, Patricia Moore, Jackie Morris, Mary Neff, Stuart Ross, Heather Smith, Catherine Stevenson, Dag T. Straumsvåg, Ingrid Waisgluss, and Suzan Yates.

Stuart Ross's fine-tuning of individual poems is exquisite. He found links to position the poems in a meaningful sequence I didn't think was possible. Thank you, Stuart.

Thanks to Lance La Rocque, Heather Smith, James McDonald, and Dag T. Straumsvåg, who directly and indirectly set me in the right direction looking for epigraphs.

Some of the poems appeared in the chapbooks *All And Everything* (Laurel Reed Books), *Small Waterways* (Apt. 9 Press), *This Close To Being A Tree* (Monk Press), *You Can't Make The Sky A Different Blue* (Big Pond Rumours), *Walking With Catherine At Lake Erie* (Shapes & Sounds Press); in leaflets published by press-press-pull/alabastine press and Puddles of Sky Press; and in the online publications Hamilton Arts & Letters, National Poetry Month (Angel House Press), and Pink Bubba Poetry.

Thanks to the editors: Kemeny Babineau, Cameron Anstee, Larry Cowan, Sharon Berg, James McDonald & Ingrid Waisgluss, Jim Clinefelter, Michael e. Casteels, Paul Lisson & Fiona Kinsella, Amanda Earl, and Daniel f. Bradley. Suzan Yates selected, edited, and arranged the poems for *You Can't Make The Sky A Different Blue*. She chose the title from a narrative that Bob Tees sent me about his visits with my late wife, Barbara Caruso, while she was in palliative care. The title is a sentence spoken by Barbara to him despite her aphasia.

Some poems were published in periodicals: *Stone the Crows!* (edited by Larry Cowan), *Illiterature* (edited by Michael e. Casteels), and the *Windsor Review*'s special issue celebrating Alice Munro (guest edited by Tim Struthers and John B. Lee for editor Marty Gervais).

Thank you, Denis De Klerck, for publishing this book. And Stuart Ross, for taking on so many tasks relating to that. Thanks to Catherine Stevenson for the cover photo, and to Laurie Siblock for the author photo.

Catherine's note about her photograph is a beautiful statement, about her process and of our friendship. Dag T. Straumsvåg's endorsement of my poetry helps push back the doubt I carry. Thank you both for contributing such supportive "Notes" to this book. I am grateful.

These poems were written 2013 to 2017. Thanks to the Ontario Arts Council for Writers' Reserve grants that enabled my writing in 2016 and 2017, and earlier.

Nelson Ball
August 20, 2017

Nelson Ball is a poet and bookseller living in Paris, Ontario. He has worked as a labourer, chauffeur, clerk, seasonal forest ranger, record store clerk, and janitor. From 1965 to 1973 he ran the legendary Weed/Flower Press, publishing mimeo editions of early books by Victor Coleman, Carol Bergé, David McFadden, bill bissett, bpNichol, and many others. He is the author of more than 40 poetry books and chapbooks.

Other Books From Mansfield Press

Poetry

Leanne Averbach, *Fever*
Tara Azzopardi, *Last Stop, Lonesome Town*
Nelson Ball, *In This Thin Rain*
Nelson Ball, *Some Mornings*
Nelson Ball, *Chewing Water*
Gary Barwin, *Moon Baboon Canoe*
Samantha Bernstein, *Spit on the Devil*
George Bowering, *Teeth: Poems 2006–2011*
Stephen Brockwell, *All of Us Reticent, Here, Together*
Stephen Brockwell, *Complete Surprising Fragments of Improbable Books*
Stephen Brockwell & Stuart Ross, eds., *Rogue Stimulus: The Stephen Harper Holiday Anthology for a Prorogued Parliament*
Diana Fitzgerald Bryden, *Learning Russian*
Alice Burdick, *Book of Short Sentences*
Alice Burdick, *Flutter*
Alice Burdick, *Holler*
Sarah Burgoyne, *Saint Twin*
Jason Camlot, *What The World Said*
Margaret Christakos, *wipe.under.a.love*
Pino Coluccio, *First Comes Love*
Marie-Ève Comtois, *My Planet of Kites*
Dani Couture, *YAW*
Gary Michael Dault, *The Milk of Birds*
Frank Davey, *Poems Suitable to Current Material Conditions*
Pier Giorgio Di Cicco, *The Dark Time of Angels*
Pier Giorgio Di Cicco, *Dead Men of the Fifties*
Pier Giorgio Di Cicco, *Early Works*
Pier Giorgio Di Cicco, *The Honeymoon Wilderness*
Pier Giorgio Di Cicco, *Living in Paradise*
Pier Giorgio Di Cicco, *My Life Without Me*
Pier Giorgio Di Cicco, *The Visible World*
Salvatore Difalco, *What Happens at Canals*
Christopher Doda, *Aesthetics Lesson*
Christopher Doda, *Among Ruins*
Christopher Doda, *Glutton for Punishment*
Glen Downie, *Monkey Soap*
Rishma Dunlop, *The Body of My Garden*
Rishma Dunlop, *Lover Through Departure: New and Selected Poems*
Rishma Dunlop, *Metropolis*
Rishma Dunlop & Priscila Uppal, eds., *Red Silk: An Anthology of South Asian Women Poets*
Puneet Dutt, *The Better Monsters*
Ollivier Dyens, *The Profane Earth*
Laura Farina, *Some Talk of Being Human*
Jaime Forsythe, *Sympathy Loophole*
Carole Glasser Langille, *Late in a Slow Time*
Eva HD, *Rotten Perfect Mouth*
Eva HD, *Shiner*
Suzanne Hancock, *Another Name for Bridge*
Jason Heroux, *Emergency Hallelujah*
Jason Heroux, *Hard Work Cheering Up Sad Machines*
Jason Heroux, *Memoirs of an Alias*
Jason Heroux, *Natural Capital*
John B. Lee, *In the Terrible Weather of Guns*
Jeanette Lynes, *The Aging Cheerleader's Alphabet*

David W. McFadden, *Abnormal Brain Sonnets*
David W. McFadden, *Be Calm, Honey*
David W. McFadden, *Shouting Your Name Down the Well: Tankas and Haiku*
David W. McFadden, *What's the Score?*
Kathryn Mockler, *The Purpose Pitch*
Leigh Nash, *Goodbye, Ukulele*
Lillian Necakov, *The Bone Broker*
Lillian Necakov, *Hooligans*
Peter Norman, *At the Gates of the Theme Park*
Peter Norman, *Water Damage*
Natasha Nuhanovic, *Stray Dog Embassy*
Catherine Owen & Joe Rosenblatt, *Dog*
Corrado Paina, *The Alphabet of the Traveler*
Corrado Paina, *Cinematic Taxi*
Corrado Paina, *The Dowry of Education*
Corrado Paina, *Hoarse Legend*
Corrado Paina, *Souls in Plain Clothes*
Nick Papaxanthos, *Love Me Tender*
Branka Petrovic, *Mechanics of a Gaze*
Stuart Ross et al., *Our Days in Vaudeville*
Matt Santateresa, *A Beggar's Loom*
Matt Santateresa, *Icarus Redux*
Ann Shin, *The Last Thing Standing*
Jim Smith, *Back Off, Assassin! New and Selected Poems*
Jim Smith, *Happy Birthday, Nicanor Parra*
Robert Earl Stewart, *Campfire Radio Rhapsody*
Robert Earl Stewart, *Something Burned along the Southern Border*
Meaghan Strimas, *Yes Or Nope*
Carey Toane, *The Crystal Palace*
Aaron Tucker, *Punchlines*
Priscila Uppal, *Sabotage*
Priscila Uppal, *Summer Sport: Poems*
Priscila Uppal, *Winter Sport: Poems*
Steve Venright, *Floors of Enduring Beauty*
Brian Wickers, *Stations of the Lost*
Tara-Michelle Ziniuk, *Whatever, Iceberg*

Fiction

Marianne Apostolides, *The Lucky Child*
Sarah Dearing, *The Art of Sufficient Conclusions*
Denis De Klerck, ed., *Particle & Wave: A Mansfield Omnibus of Electro-Magnetic Fiction*
Salvatore Difalco, *Mean Season*
Paula Eisenstein, *Flip Turn*
Sara Heinonen, *Dear Leaves, I Miss You All*
Kascia Jaronczyk, *Lemons*
Christine Miscione, *Carafola*
Marko Sijan, *Mongrel*
Tom Walmsley, *Dog Eat Rat*
Corinne Wasilewski, *Live from the Underground*

Non-Fiction

George Bowering, *How I Wrote Certain of My Books*
Denis De Klerck & Corrado Paina, eds., *College Street–Little Italy: Toronto's Renaissance Strip*
Pier Giorgio Di Cicco, *Municipal Mind: Manifestos for the Creative City*
Amy Lavender Harris, *Imagining Toronto*
David W. McFadden, *Mother Died Last Summer*
Deborah Verginella, ed., *Buon Appetito Toronto!*

For a complete list of Mansfield Press titles, please visit mansfieldpress.net